T0045525
Postcards to Paul
Talia Reed
Illustrated by Kevin Burgemeestre
CARDS

Dad and I are traveling
across the country!
We are going to visit my cousin Paul.

Dear Paul,

We are traveling through forests.

Last night we stayed in a real log cabin.

It was fun!

Ari

Paul Sorkin
12 Baker St.
West Hills, CA 91307

Hello
from
Kentucky

Dear Paul,

We saw buildings like this today.

When it's hot, people sit on their balconies in the cool shade.

Ari

Paul Sorkin
12 Baker St.
West Hills, CA 91307

Dear Paul,

We went on a
boat trip today.

We saw people
who live on the river
in houseboats!

Ari

Paul Sorkin
12 Baker St.
West Hills, CA 91307

Hi from the Mississippi!

OL MAN RIVE

Dear Paul,

We stayed at this ranch for two days.

It was a big place!

We went horseback riding.

Ari

Paul Sorkin
12 Baker St.
West Hills, CA 91307

Dear Paul,

Yesterday we saw
these cave houses.

It was hot outside,
but nice and cool inside.

See you soon!

Ari

Paul Sorkin
12 Baker St.
West Hills, CA 91307

NEW MEXICO

We drove all the next day.
We drove all the way to Paul's house.

"Hello, Paul!" I said.

"It's great to see you," said Paul.
"Thanks for your postcards!"